NASCAR RACING

The Brickyard 400

By A. R. Schaefer

Consultant:
Betty L. Carlan
Research Librarian
International Motorsports Hall of Fame
Talladega, Alabama

Capstone press

Mankato, Minnesota

Edge Books are published by Capstone Press
151 Good Counsel Drive, P.O. Box 669, Mankato, Minnesota 56002
www.capstonepress.com

Library of Congress Cataloging-in-Publication Data
Schaefer, A. R. (Adam Richard), 1976–
    The Brickyard 400 / by A.R. Schaefer.
    p. cm.—(Edge Books NASCAR racing)
    Summary: Discusses the Brickyard 400's most exciting finishes and famous racers, as
well as the history and design of the Indianapolis Motor Speedway.
    Includes bibliographical references and index.
    ISBN 0-7368-2422-7 (hardcover)
    1. Brickyard 400 (Automobile race)—Juvenile literature. [1. Brickyard 400
(Automobile race) 2. Stock car racing.] I. Title: Brickyard Four Hundred. II. Title.
III. Series.
GV1033.5.B75S35 2004
796.72—dc22   2003013440

Editorial Credits

Tom Adamson, editor; Jason Knudson, designer; Jo Miller, photo researcher

Photo Credits

Artemis Images, cover (both), 17; Indianapolis Motor Speedway, 9, 10, 11, 13, 15, 22, 25
Corbis/Bettmann, 12
Getty Images/David Taylor, 24; Robert Leberge, 5; Steve Swope, 20
SportsChrome-USA/Brian Spurlock, 18, 27, 29
Sports Gallery, Inc./Brian Spurlock, 21; Joe Robbins, 7

Table of Contents

CHAPTER 1

Making History

Stock cars roared around Indianapolis Motor Speedway (IMS) in Indianapolis, Indiana, on August 5, 2001. Jimmy Spencer started the Brickyard 400 on the pole position. He led the race for the early laps. Two-time champion Jeff Gordon started 27th out of 43 drivers.

During the beginning of the 160-lap race, Gordon was running in dirty air. He was behind a group of cars. The exhaust and airflow from these cars made his car hard to handle. He had trouble maintaining speed. Drivers can maintain their speed better when they are in the lead. Drivers in dirty air often have a hard time moving to the front.

Gordon started the 2001 race near the back of the field.

Learn about:

→ Dirty air

→ Taking the lead

→ An important race

Gordon got lucky around the 60th lap. Most drivers had to take a pit stop for fuel. But Gordon had gone into the pits earlier under a caution flag. He did not need to stop. Gordon passed most of the drivers while they were in the pits.

By the 70th lap, Gordon was in fourth place. He worked his way toward the front. When the green flag waved after a caution, Gordon went low under race leader Sterling Marlin. With 24 laps to go, Gordon was the new leader. He never gave up the lead. He raced across the finish line almost one full second ahead of Marlin. Gordon became the first driver to win three Brickyard 400s.

The Brickyard 400

The Brickyard 400 is one of NASCAR's fastest races. The history and reputation of IMS make this 400-mile (644-kilometer) race one of the most important races on NASCAR's schedule. Every driver wants to win at this track.

Gordon savored his record third Brickyard win.

Indianapolis Motor Speedway

Indianapolis Motor Speedway is one of the most famous racetracks in the world. It is best known as the home of the Indianapolis 500. The track has more than 250,000 seats. IMS is the biggest sports facility in the world.

Track Design

The design of the racetrack is simple. The track is a rectangle with rounded corners. The track is 2.5 miles (4 kilometers) long. The frontstretch and backstretch are each .625 mile (1 kilometer) long. The two sides are called short chutes. They are .125 mile (.2 kilometer) long.

"You have to be good through the corners, good down the straightaways, you have to be good everywhere there."
—Jeff Gordon, sportsillustrated.cnn.com, 8-1-02

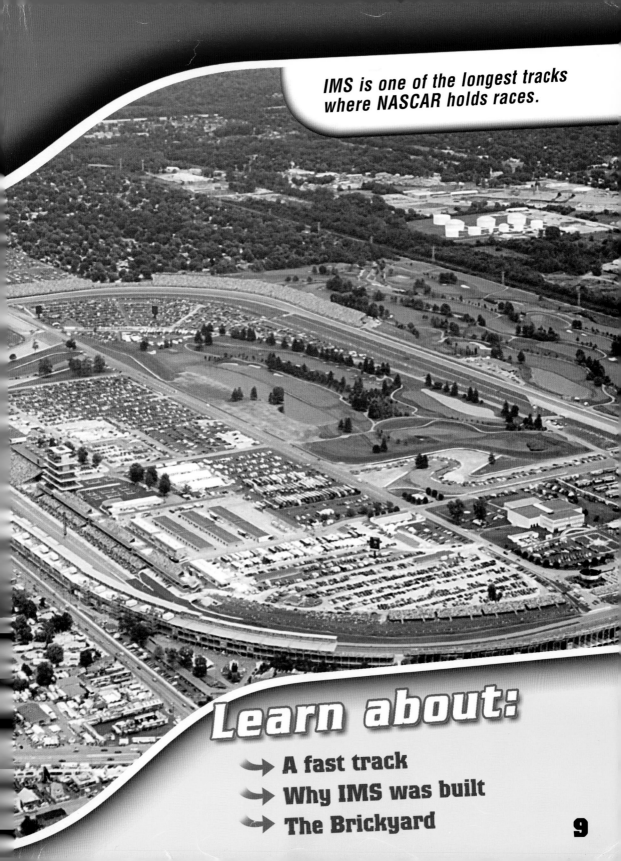

IMS is one of the longest tracks where NASCAR holds races.

Learn about:

→ A fast track

→ Why IMS was built

→ The Brickyard

9

Cars can build up speed on the long frontstretch.

Each of the four turns is 440 yards (402 meters) long. The turns are banked at a little more than 9 degrees. This banking is low compared to other NASCAR tracks.

NASCAR drivers can go very fast on the track's long straightaways. They can reach 200 miles (320 kilometers) an hour on the frontstretch and backstretch. Drivers slow down for the corners because of the low banks. But the corners are not very tight. They can still take the corners fast.

The corners at IMS are only banked slightly.

History of IMS

Four Indiana business owners paid to have IMS built in 1909. During the early 1900s, many cars were being built in Indiana. Car companies tested their new cars on the track. The business owners also wanted the companies to race their cars. They thought these races would increase the companies' sales.

The track at the Brickyard was once paved with bricks.

The Yard of Bricks remains at the start-finish line.

The track was built out of crushed rocks held together with tar. People soon learned that this surface was not good for racing. In fall 1909, the track was repaved with 3.2 million bricks. The bricks gave the racetrack its nickname, "The Brickyard."

By 1961, the bricks were covered with pavement. A row of the original bricks remains at the start-finish line. The row is called the Yard of Bricks.

"There are a lot of things about going to Indy that are really cool. It's neat because of all the history there."
—Matt Kenseth, sportsillustrated.cnn.com, 8-1-02

TRACK DIAGRAM
Indianapolis Motor Speedway

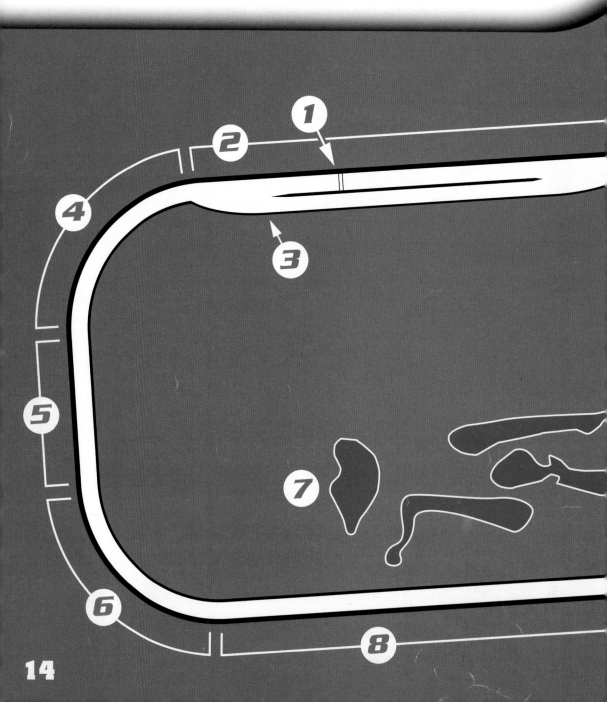

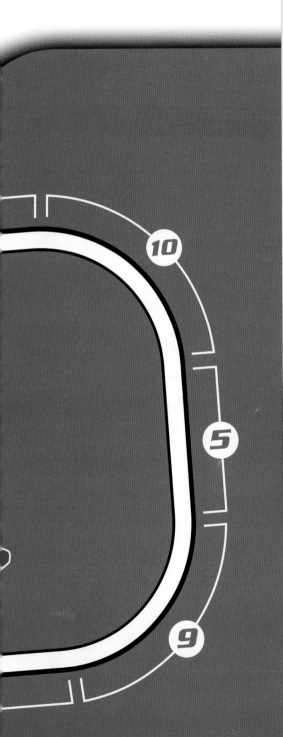

1. Start-finish line
2. Frontstretch
3. Pit road
4. Turn 1
5. Short chutes
6. Turn 2
7. Brickyard Crossing Golf Course
8. Backstretch
9. Turn 3
10. Turn 4

CHAPTER 3

Famous Races

IMS is home to three major races. The Brickyard 400, the Indianapolis 500, and the U.S. Grand Prix are held at IMS. Only the Brickyard is a NASCAR race. The Indianapolis 500 is part of the Indy Racing League. The U.S. Grand Prix is part of the Formula One series. Indy cars and Formula One cars look very different from stock cars. They can go faster than stock cars, but they look less like regular cars.

For the track's first 85 years, the only major race was the Indy 500. The first Brickyard 400 was in 1994. The first U.S. Grand Prix at IMS was held in 2000.

Formula One cars race at IMS during the U.S. Grand Prix.

Learn about:

→ Greatest Spectacle in Racing
→ A landmark victory
→ The closest 400 ever

The Indy 500 is one of the most popular races in the world.

The Indianapolis 500

During the first few years of racing in Indianapolis, not many people went to the races. The races usually took several days. The owners thought that they should try one big race.

The first Indianapolis 500-Mile Race was on May 30, 1911. The winner received $14,250. This race was the start of the longest car racing tradition in the United States. The Indy 500 always takes place on Memorial Day weekend. Today, the 500 is known as the "Greatest Spectacle in Racing," and the winner takes home millions of dollars.

"It's impossible to put into words how much the Indy 500 means to me. It is still the one victory I'd most like to have."
—Tony Stewart, *True Speed: My Racing Life*, 2002

The First Brickyard

The Indy 500 was the only major race held at IMS until 1994. In February 1993, the presidents of NASCAR and IMS announced that a new race would take place in Indianapolis in August 1994. The new stock car race was named the Brickyard 400.

Jeff Gordon won the first Brickyard 400 in 1994.

Jeff Gordon

Jeff Gordon is one of the most popular drivers in NASCAR. Even people who do not follow racing recognize his rainbow-colored car.

Gordon grew up in California and started racing go-karts when he was a kid. When he was about 13, his family moved to Indiana. They thought Gordon would have more racing opportunities there. The family lived near Indianapolis Motor Speedway. Gordon dreamed of racing at IMS.

Gordon drove in his first Winston Cup race in 1992 when he was 21 years old. Gordon's breakout year was 1994. He won two races, including the first Brickyard 400. During the next seven seasons, Gordon won the NASCAR championship four times. He also won two more Brickyards, in 1998 and 2001.

Gordon won 61 races in his first 10 seasons in NASCAR's top racing division. He is expected to be a winning driver for many more years.

People were not sure what to expect at the first race. Stock cars had never raced at IMS before. Hundreds of thousands of fans bought tickets to see what would happen. The race was a huge success. Jeff Gordon was just 23 years old, but he won the first Brickyard 400 in front of more than 250,000 people. Almost overnight, the Brickyard 400 became one of the most important races in NASCAR.

Gordon passes traffic during the 1998 race.

The Brickyard 400

Race Statistics

Year	Driver	Car	Starting Position	Prize Money
1994	Jeff Gordon	Chevrolet	3	$613,000
1995	Dale Earnhardt	Chevrolet	13	$565,600
1996	Dale Jarrett	Ford	24	$564,035
1997	Ricky Rudd	Ford	7	$571,000
1998	Jeff Gordon	Chevrolet	3	$637,625
1999	Dale Jarrett	Ford	4	$712,240
2000	Bobby Labonte	Pontiac	3	$831,225
2001	Jeff Gordon	Chevrolet	27	$428,452
2002	Bill Elliott	Dodge	2	$449,056
2003	Kevin Harvick	Chevrolet	1	$418,253

Blink of an Eye

In 1997, the Brickyard 400 was a close race. The lead changed 19 times during the race. Gordon and Dale Jarrett were each trying for their second title. Gordon and Jarrett led the pack when they went into the pits for fuel with 14 laps to go.

Ricky Rudd thought he had enough fuel to finish the race without going into the pits. He was right. Jarrett and Gordon dropped to third and fourth. The race came down to Rudd and Bobby Labonte. Rudd raced across the finish line just ahead of Labonte. Rudd won the race by 0.183 second. The race was the closest Brickyard 400 ever.

"It's by far the biggest race I've ever won. It means as much to me as I've ever accomplished on the racetrack before."
—Ricky Rudd, my.brickyard.com, 4-7-98

Rudd battled Labonte for the win in 1997.

CHAPTER 4

Famous Racers

Most of the world's most famous drivers have competed at IMS at least once. All major racing circuits now run there. All of NASCAR's stars in the 1990s and 2000s have raced at Indianapolis. Jeff Gordon and Dale Jarrett have won the 400 more than once.

Dale Earnhardt

Dale Earnhardt was one of the most famous NASCAR drivers of all time. He won the series championship seven times in 15 years. He won 76 NASCAR races during his career. In 1979, he was the NASCAR Rookie of the Year and won the championship the next year. Many people say that he was the best NASCAR driver ever.

Earnhardt was one of the legends who have won the Brickyard 400.

Learn about:

→ Dale Earnhardt

→ Bill Elliott

→ Legendary track

27

Earnhardt raced in the Brickyard 400 seven times. He finished in the top 10 five times. In 1995, he won the race by beating another NASCAR legend, Rusty Wallace. Earnhardt died in a crash on the final lap of the Daytona 500 in 2001.

Bill Elliott

Bill Elliott was one of the best NASCAR drivers in the 1980s. He is also one of the most popular drivers ever. Elliott finished in the top six of the season standings every year from 1983 to 1990. In 1985, he won 11 races. He won the NASCAR championship in 1988.

Elliott has raced in every Brickyard 400. He came close to winning several times. He finished third in 1994 and 2000. He finished fourth in 1995. He scored four top-10 finishes in other years. In 2002, Elliott won his first Brickyard 400 at age 46.

"This is the greatest, the greatest win of my career."

—Bill Elliott, sportsillustrated.cnn.com, 8-4-02

The IMS Legend

The history and legend of Indianapolis Motor Speedway make the Brickyard 400 one of the most important NASCAR races every year. The high speeds on the straightaways make the race exciting for fans. Most drivers consider it an honor just to race at the Brickyard.

Elliott took home the Brickyard 400 trophy in 2002.

Glossary

backstretch (BAK-strech)—the straight part of a racetrack that is opposite the frontstretch

bank (BANGK)—the angle of the track; if a track has a high bank, the top of the track is much taller than the bottom of the track.

caution (KAW-shun)—a time during a race when drivers have to slow down and are not allowed to pass; a caution occurs after a crash or when the track crew has to clean up debris.

dirty air (DURT-ee AIR)—the exhaust and airflow behind race cars on the track

exhaust (eg-ZAWST)—the waste gases produced by a car's engine

frontstretch (FRUHNT-strech)—the straight part of a racetrack where the race begins and ends

pole (POHL)—the inside spot at the front of the line at the beginning of a race

straightaway (STRAY-tuh-way)—a long, straight part of a racetrack

tradition (truh-DISH-uhn)—an event that has been held every year for many years

Read More

Dubois, Muriel. *Pro Stock Cars*. Wild Rides! Mankato, Minn.: Capstone Press, 2002.

Johnstone, Michael. *NASCAR*. The Need for Speed. Minneapolis: LernerSports, 2002.

Woods, Bob. *Dirt Track Daredevils: The History of NASCAR*. World of NASCAR. Excelsior, Minn.: Tradition Books, 2003.

Useful Addresses

Indianapolis Motor Speedway
4790 West 16th Street
Indianapolis, IN 46222

International Motorsports Hall of Fame
P.O. Box 1018
Talladega, AL 35161

NASCAR
P.O. Box 2875
Daytona Beach, FL 32120

Internet Sites

FactHound offers a safe, fun way to find Internet sites related to this book. All of the sites on FactHound have been researched by our staff.

Here's how:

1. Visit *www.facthound.com*
2. Type in this special code **0736824227** for age-appropriate sites. Or enter a search word related to this book for a more general search.
3. Click on the **Fetch It** button.

FactHound will fetch the best sites for you!

Index